ST. GREGORY THE GREAT

The Life and Miracles of St. Benedict

Translated by Carl A. Vater, PhD
With an introduction by Jerome C. Foss, PhD

ASCENSION
West Chester, Pennsylvania

© 2024 Ascension Publishing Group, LLC. All rights reserved.

With the exception of short excerpts used in articles and critical reviews, no part of this work may be reproduced, transmitted, or stored in any form whatsoever, printed or electronic, without the prior written permission of the publisher.

Scripture quotations are from the Revised Standard Version of the Bible–Second Catholic Edition (Ignatius Edition) © 2006 National Council of the Churches of Christ in the United States of America. Used by permission. All rights reserved.

Ascension
PO Box 1990
West Chester, PA 19380
1-800-376-0520
ascensionpress.com

Cover design: James Kegley

Printed in the United States of America
24 25 26 27 28 5 4 3 2 1

ISBN: 978-1-935940-36-4

For the Students of Saint Vincent College

Venite, filii; audite me:
timorem Domini docebo vos.
—*Psalm 33:12* [1]

---

[1] This verse is numbered as Psalm 34:11 in most English translations of the Bible.

CONTENTS

About the Catholic Classics 1

Introduction to St. Gregory the Great's
Life and Miracles of St. Benedict by Jerome C. Foss 3

Preface 9

Chapter 1: On the Broken and Mended Colander 11

Chapter 2: On Overcoming a Temptation of the Flesh 15

Chapter 3: On the Glass Bottle Broken at the Sign of the Cross 17

Chapter 4: On Returning a Wayward Monk to Salvation 22

Chapter 5: On the Water Which He Produced
from the Rock on Top of the Mountain 24

Chapter 6: On the Return of the Iron to
the Handle from the Depths of the Water 26

Chapter 7: On His Disciple, Who Walked Upon
the Waters with His Feet 28

Chapter 8: Of the Poisoned Bread Carried Far Off by the Raven 30

Chapter 9: On the Removal of a Large Stone Through His Prayer 35

Chapter 10: On the Imaginary Flame in the Kitchen 36

Chapter 11: On the Crushed and Healed Little Servant of God 37

Chapter 12: On the Monks Who Ate Outside the Kitchen 39

Chapter 13: On the Brother of Valentinian
Who Also Ate Outside the Kitchen 41

Chapter 14: On Catching King Totila's Subterfuge 43

Chapter 15: On the Prophecy Made About King Totila 45

Chapter 16: On the Cleric Liberated from a Demon 47

Chapter 17: On the Prophecy of His Monastery's Destruction 51

Chapter 18: On the Flagon Cast Off and Known through the Spirit 53

Chapter 19: On the Napkins Received by the Servant of God 54

Chapter 20: On the Knowledge of an Arrogant Boy
Known Through the Spirit 55

Chapter 21: On the Two Hundred Measures of Flour
Found Outside His Cell in Time of Famine . . . . : 56

Chapter 22: On the Vision by Which He Commanded
the Building of the Monastery in Terracina 58

Chapter 23: On the Handmaidens of God Who Returned
to Communion After Their Death by His Offering 60

Chapter 24: Of the Young Monk Whom
the Earth Cast from His Grave 63

Chapter 25: On the Monk Who Found a Dragon
Against Him on the Way 64

Chapter 26: On the Boy Cured of Leprosy 65

Chapter 27: On the Gold Coins Returned
to a Debtor Through a Miracle 66

Chapter 28: On the Glass Bottle Thrown
Against the Rock and Not Broken 68

Chapter 29: On the Large Jug Emptied and Filled with Oil 70

Chapter 30: On a Monk Liberated from a Demon 71

Chapter 31: On the Bound Farmer Released
by Benedict's Sight Alone 73

Chapter 32: On the Raising of the Dead 76

Chapter 33: On his Sister Scholastica's Miracle 78

Chapter 34: On the Vision of His Sister's Soul
and How It Departed from Her Body 81

Chapter 35: On the World Gathered Before His Eyes
and On the Soul of Germanus, Bishop of Capua 82

Chapter 36: On the Writing of the Rule for Monks 85

Chapter 37: On the Prophecy of His Death Foretold to the Brothers 86

Chapter 38: Of the Insane Woman Healed Through His Cave 88

The text of *The Life and Miracles of St. Benedict* in this book was translated from *S. Gregorii Magni Dialogorum Liber Secundus de Vita et Miraculis S. Benedicti* in *Vita et Regula SS. P. Benedicti* (Cincinnati, 1880), 1–76, for use in the Saint Vincent College Core Curriculum.

ABOUT THE CATHOLIC CLASSICS

There are texts by great saints that many devout Catholics are convinced they should read, but perhaps they feel overwhelmed by the thought. Most of these texts were originally written in a foreign language centuries ago. The available English translations often use terminology that has fallen out of use, making them more challenging to the modern reader. One can leave such texts with more questions than answers. They can seem unapproachable to all but scholars.

But these writings were intended as gifts to all of God's faithful so that we can know more *about* God and, more importantly, so that we can *know* God. Each saint, each Doctor of the Church, each mystic reflects some aspect of the beauty and goodness of our creator.

To help renew Catholics' appreciation of these works, Ascension has created this series, Catholic Classics. With updated translations, the works are more readable to modern eyes. Added introductions and commentary help unlock the text and give context to the original author's references.

The peacock is the symbol for the Catholic Classics. It is an ancient Christian symbol of eternal life and the resurrection that reflects the perennial nature of these classics and the new life they will breathe into your spiritual life as you read them. The Scriptures tell us that King Solomon, renowned for his wisdom, kept peacocks, which were a mark of his grandeur (1 Kings 10:22). The peacock evokes the great wisdom contained in these classic works.

As you read, remember to use this opportunity as a moment of encounter with the living God. Pray as you read. See Christ in the words of his servants—of his friends—and know that he waits there for you.

Introduction

You hold before you a great work of the Catholic intellectual tradition that, next to *The Rule of St. Benedict*, has been shaping monastic life and thinking for well over a millennium. It is also a great work of the liberal arts tradition. St. Gregory the Great's account of St. Benedict's life is a book that both instructs the faithful and teases the scholarly. This new translation by Carl Vater, philosophy professor at Saint Vincent College in Latrobe, Pennsylvania, is intended to facilitate a close reading of the text that is both holy and intelligent.

Those of us interested in the monastic tradition owe a debt of gratitude to St. Gregory, for it is thanks to his masterful and engaging book that we have biographical stories of St. Benedict that continue to be shared in monasteries throughout the world. As you will read, Benedict, who was born in the year 480, was sent to Rome for school but found his studies and peers to be too worldly. As a result, he retreated into the countryside to devote himself to prayer. After three years living as a hermit, he was providentially called to serve as a spiritual father for others seeking a similar way of life. Later, he founded monasteries in the mountainous wildernesses of central Italy, in places such as Monte Cassino, where he died in the year 543.

Benedict is remembered for the many miracles that were brought about through his prayers and the gifts given to him by the Holy Spirit so that he might better fulfill his unique vocation. But the most memorable miracle of the book belongs to his twin sister, Scholastica, and I will not spoil it by retelling it here. It is one of the most famous stories of the book!

Thanks to Gregory's efforts, many Catholics today know more about Benedict than they do about Gregory himself. Younger by half a century or so, Gregory led a life that parallelled Benedict's in several respects. Both men were born into noble families but gave up their prestigious futures for the more contemplative life of a monk. And in both cases, Divine Providence desired lives of responsibility from these exceptional men of faith. Gregory was the first monk to be called to serve as pope, a position he took in 590 and held until his death in 604. One would have great difficulty overstating the importance of his papacy. His liturgical reforms remain important to this day, including the liturgical chant that adopted the name Gregorian. Around 595, he sent St. Augustine of Canterbury to Britain to convert the king and people from the errors of paganism. Closer to home, Gregory organized a massive system of relief for the poor, which provided food and other necessities to the many refugees living in Rome. It was to Gregory's credit more than any mere political figure that Rome survived that difficult period. Few have been more deserving of the title "Great."

Not only is Gregory a remarkable saint, but he is also one of the Latin Fathers and Doctors of the Church, thanks to his astute learning and prolific writing. His *Book of Pastoral Care*, for instance, is considered a classic text and useful for guiding all in busy leadership positions. But none of his books are quite equal to *The Dialogues*. Indeed, in some circles, this great text has earned him the name "Gregory Dialogos," or Gregory the Dialogist.

Gregory's *Dialogues*, which contain *The Life and Miracles of St. Benedict*, would likely be understood by most readers today as a collection of hagiographies, pious biographies of saints. But as the title suggests, Gregory himself intended the four volumes that compose the work to be a classical dialogue in which characters are in conversation with one another. Plato's dialogues are the most well-known in this genre. Cicero and St. Augustine also wrote dialogues, and theirs are better examples of precursors to Gregory's, for like them Gregory is the main character and does most of the talking. Gregory's words are directed at an educated deacon named Peter who wishes to learn more about famous monks of sixth-century Italy. The only one to receive a volume of stories unto himself is St. Benedict, whose life and miracles are presented in volume 2. This volume is often printed on its own, as it is here, and goes under the title *The Life and Miracles of St. Benedict*.

The format gives us a good indication of the intended audience for *The Dialogues*. Gregory is hoping his writing helps those like Deacon Peter, who have a strong faith and a working knowledge of the Bible, come to a deeper understanding of human cooperation with Divine Providence, or what we might call sanctified leadership. This explains the reason for the book's continued popularity with reflective Catholics today who are eager to think more carefully about their own vocations. The extended discussion of Benedict has long been useful for those seeking deeper holiness in the busy workaday world of modern times. This is as true for the laity as it is for today's monks who follow Benedict's footsteps most closely.

My own recommendation in reading Gregory's *Life and Miracles of St. Benedict* is to take Deacon Peter as your fellow student, your partner in working through the events that make the story of Benedict so memorable. When Peter asks Gregory for an explanation, you should pause and ask yourself if Peter's question is your question. In most cases, you will probably find that it is. Peter helps us see when we should dig in deeper and reflect with greater care. He is a literary device Gregory provides to help us better understand what we are reading and why it matters.

I also recommend paying attention to the general organization of Benedict's story as told by Gregory. This will likely mean reading the text more than once. The first time through gives many the impression that most of the story is a compilation of miracles that have little to do with one another other than amassing evidence of Benedict's holiness. If the organization is not accounted for, then the miracles have the effect that the poorer kinds of hagiography have, which is to make the saints seem superhuman and unapproachable. Gregory's intention is quite the opposite. The miracles are meant to draw us in, but the story's arc teaches us that Benedict is on a journey of sanctification—just like all of us. His life is a progression from good intentions to a fuller understanding of the human condition, an understanding that is crucial for the development of our earthly and heavenly relationships.

To give some indication of Benedict's progress without spoiling the fun of reading it for yourself, I suggest taking note of his early retreat from the world and his youthful desire for perfection which he seeks in the isolation of a cave. After a period of time comparable to that which young men and women spend in college today, God calls Benedict to serve as a leader. His response to this call is marked by several temptations and trials, all of which he overcomes. He is led to Monte Cassino, where he completes his *Rule* and serves as the spiritual father of many. His maturity at this point is noted by the secular world as much as by the faithful; he is even paid a visit by an invading king. But Benedict's own growth is not complete. We learn from the story of Scholastica that she understands more deeply that rules matter but can never replace the ends to which they point. Learning from her, Benedict ends his days not in isolation but in greater communion with his fellow monks, at which point he is prepared for the communion we are given through Christ's death and Resurrection.

Carl Vater's translation of this timeless classic is meant to facilitate our own thoughtful response to God's call in each of our lives. To sit and read a great book like the one you hold is to retire, if temporarily, from the business of the workaday world, to escape to the wilderness where we can pray. *The Life and Miracles of St. Benedict* thus serves as a reminder and an example of what a liberal arts education should be—a temporary retreat from the world that we might be better prepared to live out our vocations as men and women of God.

One of the great mottos of the Benedictines is *Ora et Labora*, Pray and Work. This balance that has guided monasteries for so long has also been embraced by people called to serve in ways that require greater integration with the secular world. Gregory shows us that while not everyone can build a monastery atop a mountain, everyone can be more like St. Benedict!

—Jerome C. Foss

Preface

GREGORY:[1] There was a man of venerable life blessed by the grace of God and blessed in name—Benedict.[2] He bore a mature heart even from the time of his youth and gave his soul no wicked pleasure, since his way of life passed beyond his age.[3] But while he was still on this earth, which he could have freely used, he despised the world as if it were a desert world with fruit.[4] He was born in the province of Nursia to free parents, and he was sent to Rome to study the liberal arts. But when he discerned that many in these studies descend into a life of vice, he withdrew his foot, which he could have set forth into the world, so that he might not also entirely fall into the huge pit[5] after attaining some of this knowledge. Therefore, with contempt for the study of the liberal arts, he left his father's home and affairs and, desiring to please God alone, he sought a life of holy contemplation. Thus, he left Rome knowingly ignorant and wisely untaught. I did not learn all the details of his life, but the few that I recount to you I learned from four of his disciples, namely, from the most reverend Constantine, who succeeded him

---

1 St. Gregory the Great wrote this work as a dialogue. Throughout most of the text, he is the speaker.
2 St. Benedict's name in Latin is *Benedictus*, which means "blessed." Thus, St. Gregory the Great is opening this part of his dialogues with a pun: literally, "There was a man *Blessed* by the grace of God and in name."
3 "Age" (*aetatem*) has a double meaning here. St. Benedict's way of life passed beyond both his physical age and beyond the customs of his time.
4 The phrase "desert world with fruit" seems to use the metaphor of fruit to refer to the allure of worldly things that are good for food, a delight to the eyes, and desirable for wisdom but are not profitable for salvation (see Genesis 3:6).
5 See Revelation 9:1–2 where hell is likened to a bottomless pit.

as abbot in the monastery; from Valentinian, too, who presided over Lateran Abbey for many years; from Simplicius, who ruled over the congregation third after him; and from Honoratus, who is now presiding over that abbey in which he first began to live a monastic life.

CHAPTER 1

On the Broken and Mended Colander

Once he had abandoned his studies and resolved to seek out the desert, his nurse, who loved him dearly, was the only one who followed him. And when they arrived at the place called Effide, they stayed in the church of St. Peter with many worthy men who received him there with charity. One day his nurse borrowed a colander for cleaning wheat from the neighbor women, and it accidentally broke into two pieces when it was left unguarded on the table. Then his nurse began to cry vehemently because she saw that the utensil she had borrowed was broken. But when he saw his nurse crying, Benedict, a religious and pious boy, moved with compassion for her sorrow, took both broken pieces away with him and prayed with tears in his eyes. And rising from his prayer, he found that the vessel was already so thoroughly fixed that no one could find a trace of where it had been broken. He returned the mended colander, which he had taken broken, to his nurse, consoling her soothingly. This event is known to everyone in that place and is held in such admiration that they hung the colander at the entrance to the church for the inhabitants of that place, so that all, both the living and their children, may know that the boy Benedict began his life of conversion from such a state of perfection. The colander was before the eyes of all the people there for many years, even until the time of the Lombards, hanging over the church door.

But Benedict, desiring to be dragged through the evils of this world more than to receive praises, to be fatigued for work of God more than to be extolled for the benefits of this life, fleeing his nurse secretly sought out a secluded place in the wilderness called Subiaco, which is about four miles from the city of Rome. There is a cool, clear fountain that flows forth from there, forms a broad lake, and afterwards flows into a river. As he traveled in his flight, a monk named Romanus met him and asked him where he was going. Romanus came to know his desires, kept them secret, gave him aid and frequent holy conversation, and ministered to him as much as he could.

Having arrived in Subiaco, the man of God spent three years in a narrow cave entirely hidden from all except for the monk Romanus. Romanus lived in a monastery nearby under the rule of Abbot[6] Adeodatus. Romanus would piously sneak away for hours from under the eyes of his Abbot, and he was able to steal some bread that was given for him to eat and carry it to Benedict. There was no path from Romanus' cell[7] to the cave because a lofty cliff projected above the cave. So, Romanus used to lower the bread from the clifftop tied to a rope. He also tied a little bell to the rope so that at the sound of the bell the man of God would know when Romanus was offering bread, which he would go out and get. But when the ancient Enemy, jealous of one's charity for the refreshment of another, spied the bread being lowered one day, he threw a stone and broke the little bell. Nevertheless, Romanus did not cease to minister to Benedict at those convenient hours.

---

6   Literally, this word in Latin is "Father" (*pater*). It is translated "Abbot" since that is the term used for the head of a monastery in contemporary English.
7   A monk's "cell" is his bedroom in the monastery.

But when Almighty God willed for Romanus to rest from his labor and to demonstrate Benedict's life as an example to men so that, as a lamp placed on a lampstand might shine,[8] he might shine for all who are in God's house, he deigned to appear to a certain priest staying a long way off, who had prepared his Easter dinner. And God said to the priest, "You have prepared delights for yourself, and my servant is afflicted with hunger in his place." The priest immediately arose[9] and on Easter day itself went to the place with the food he had prepared for himself and searched for the man of God through steep mountains, hollow valleys, and underground pits. He found him hidden in a cave, and when they had prayed together, they sat down together, blessing Almighty God. And after a sweet conversation about life, the priest said to Benedict, "Rise up! Let us eat this food because today is the feast of Easter!" The man of God answered him, saying, "I know that it is the feast of Easter because I have merited to see you." Since he had been so long removed from men, he did not know that day was the feast of Easter. But the venerable priest again assured him, saying, "Truly, today is Easter Sunday of the Resurrection. It is unfitting for you to fast because I have been sent to you so that we may eat the gifts of the Lord Almighty together!" Therefore, blessing God, they ate the food. When they finished their meal and conversation, the priest returned to his church.

At the same time, shepherds discovered him hidden in the cave. Since they saw him dressed in animal pelts among the bushes, some believed him to be a beast, but coming to know the servant of God, many of them changed their lives from a bestial mind to the grace of piety. Thus, his name became known in the whole area, and from that time on he began to be visited by many people,

---

8   See Mark 4:21–25.
9   "Arose" is a translation of *surrexit*, which is one of the Latin words used for Christ's Resurrection.

who carried up the food of the body to him and carried back from his mouth spiritual nourishment[10] in their breasts.

---

10 Literally, "the nourishment of life" (*alimentum ... vitae*).

CHAPTER 2

On Overcoming a Temptation of the Flesh

On a certain day, the Tempter was present while Benedict was alone. A small, dark bird, which is commonly called a blackbird, began to fly near his face and annoyingly continued flying in his face so that the holy man could have grabbed it with his hand if he wanted to. But the bird departed, sent away by the Sign of the Cross.

And there followed the departure of the bird a temptation of the flesh stronger than any the holy man had ever experienced. For there was a certain woman that he had sometimes seen, whom an evil spirit brought back to his mind's eye, and the servant of God's mind was so aroused that the flame of lust caught fire in his breast before he could stop it. He thought about quitting his wilderness way of life for the sake of pleasure. But immediately he came back to himself by heavenly grace, and seeing a thicket overflowing with nettles and thornbushes, he stripped off his garments and threw himself into the stinging spines and burning nettles. He wallowed there until his whole body was wounded when he got out of the bush, and he removed a wound of the mind through the wounds of his skin because pleasure is dragged away in pain. And since he burned the temptation externally in bodily punishment, he extinguished what illicitly burned internally. Thus, he conquered sin because he changed the fire. From that time, as he later told his disciples, the temptation of pleasure was so subdued in him that he barely felt anything in such a temptation.

Afterwards, many people also began to leave the world and hasten to his teaching. Of course, free from the vice of temptation, he had become by right a master of virtues. Consequently, in the Exodus, Moses advised that the Levites ought to minister from the age of twenty-five, but they became guardians of the holy vessels at fifty.[11]

PETER: Some of what you say is clear to me, but still, it would be clearer from more explanation.[12]

GREGORY: It is plain, Peter, that the temptation of the flesh is hot in youth, but the heat of the body cools beginning at fifty. And the minds of the faithful are sacred vessels. Therefore, God's chosen servants must serve and be fatigued in obedience and toil when they are in the midst of temptation. But when the heat of temptation returns to a tranquil state of mind, they are guardians of the holy vessels because they become teachers of souls.

PETER: What you say satisfies me. But since you have unlocked the lock of his life to this point, I ask that you explain the rest of that just man's life.

GREGORY: By withdrawing from temptation, the man of God, like a field plowed by the rooting up of thorns, gave true fruit in a land of virtues. Thus, his name was famous, and his extraordinary way of life was praised.

---

11 See Numbers 8:23–26.
12 To this point in the text, the dialogue has been entirely one-sided. Now, the interlocutor, Peter, begins to have a more active role in the conversation.

CHAPTER 3

On the Glass Bottle Broken at the Sign of the Cross

There was a nearby monastery where the abbot had died. All the monks from that congregation came to the venerable Benedict and begged him with intense requests that he ought to rule over them. Every day he sent them off with his refusal, predicting that his customs and those of the brothers could not agree, but when at last he was conquered by their requests, he gave his assent to rule over them.

The monks had previously fallen from the path to the left and to the right through illicit acts, but since he now had the care of the regular life in that monastery, Benedict permitted no monk to fall away from the journey of daily conversion. Perceiving this about Benedict, the brothers began to rage insanely, first beginning to accuse themselves since they had asked him to rule over them and his fortitude in the standard of rectitude displeased them.

They saw that under him illicit acts were not permitted, and it grieved them to give up their accustomed way of life. With their old way of thinking, it was hard for them to be turned to new ways of thinking. The life of the good is always burdensome for those with depraved behavior, so some of them tried to arrange for Benedict's death. Their first plan was to mix poison in his wine.

When they offered the glass with that deadly drink to their abbot, who was reclining at table for blessing, as was the custom of the monastery, Benedict made the Sign of the Cross with his hand outstretched. And the glass, which was held a ways off from him, broke at the Sign of the Cross and was so shattered that it was as if he had thrown a stone at that vessel of death with the Cross.

The man of God understood immediately that it could not carry the sign of life since it had a drink of death. He arose from his place with a placid expression and tranquil mind, and he admonished the assembled brothers, saying, "May God have mercy on you, brothers. Why did you want to do this to me? Did I not tell you before that your customs and mine did not agree? Go and seek for yourselves another abbot who is in accord with your customs because you cannot have me as your abbot after this." Then, he returned to his place of beloved solitude and dwelt alone with himself before the eyes of his heavenly Spectator.

PETER: I do not understand clearly what "he dwelt with himself" means.

GREGORY: If the holy man, contrary to his own mind, had wished to have under him daily those men conspiring against him and quite unlike him in way of life, perhaps it would have been beyond his strength and his manner of tranquility, and perhaps it would have turned aside the eye of his mind from the light of contemplation. And when he was fatigued with their daily correction, he might care for himself less. Perhaps he would have lost himself and not found them. For as often as we are directed outside ourselves excessively by our train of thought, we are ourselves but we are not with ourselves because we wander about through others' affairs barely seeing ourselves. Do we say that the man was with himself who departed for a far-off region, ate the portion of his inheritance he was given, was hired by a citizen in that region, and cared for the pigs, whose pods he saw and hungered to eat?[13] Yet, when he later began to think of the good things he squandered, it is written of him: "But when he came to himself he said, 'How many of my father's hired servants have bread enough and to spare?'"[14] If he was with himself, how did he come to himself? Therefore, I said that the venerable man dwelt with himself because in always surveying himself, always regarding himself before the eyes of his Maker, always examining himself, he never turned the eye of his soul away from himself.

PETER: What about what is written of the apostle Peter, when he was led out from prison by an angel? Because when he had returned to himself, he said: "Now I am sure that the Lord has sent his angel and rescued me from the hand of Herod and from all that the Jewish people were expecting."[15]

GREGORY: We are led outside ourselves in two ways, Peter. For either we are pulled beneath ourselves through a lapse in thinking, or we are raised above ourselves through the grace of contemplation. The one who fed the pigs fell beneath himself through the wandering and foulness of his mind. The one whom the angel released and whose mind was rapt in ecstasy was truly outside himself, but he was above himself. Therefore, each one returns to himself: the former draws himself to his heart from the error of his deeds and the latter returns from the height of contemplation to the general understanding he had before. Therefore, venerable Benedict dwelled with himself in that solitude insofar as he guarded himself behind the door of contemplation. For whenever the fire of contemplation caught him up into the heights,[16] without a doubt he left himself below himself.

---

13 St. Gregory is referring to the parable of the Prodigal Son. See Luke 15:11–32.
14 Luke 15:17.
15 Acts 12:11.
16 See 2 Corinthians 12:2, where St. Paul says he knows of a man of Christ who was "caught up to the third heaven."

PETER: I am satisfied by what you say, but I ask that you tell me if he ought to have deserted the brothers once he had accepted them.

GREGORY: I think, Peter, that evil men may be endured patiently in a community where we find some men who will be helpful for a good man. For where the fruit of good men is entirely lacking, sometimes labor spent on bad men becomes useless, especially if God's call for the good man to bear better fruit elsewhere is strong enough. Therefore, what reason would drive the holy man to continue his care over those who unanimously decided to persecute him? And we should not pass over in silence that the perfect always bear in mind that when they consider their labor to be without fruit, they move to another place so that they may labor fruitfully.

Consequently, that extraordinary preacher, who longed to be dissolved and to be with Christ, to whom "to live is Christ, and to die is gain,"[17] who not only desired the battle of sufferings for himself but also desired to set others on fire to tolerate sufferings as well, got a rope and basket and desired to be lowered secretly from the city wall when he was persecuted in Damascus.[18] Should we say that Paul feared death, a death he desired in order to testify to the love of Jesus? No! But when he saw the little fruit that was available to him in that place even by great labor, he turned his labor elsewhere where he might have fruit. And, indeed, this mighty soldier of God was unwilling to be held back behind the gate; he sought out battle on the plain. Consequently, you will recognize right away, if you listen closely, that in the same way venerable Benedict did not desert the unteachable men living there so much as he raised up the souls of other men from death in other places.

---

17   St. Gregory is referring to St. Paul. See Philippians 1:21.
18   Acts of the Apostles 9:23–25.

PETER: It is as you teach me, and both clear reason and the testimony of Paul declare it. But I ask that you return to the story of the life of such a great abbot where you left off.

GREGORY: When the holy man grew daily in virtues and the working of miracles in that same wilderness, many men gathered around him in that place to serve Almighty God. So with the help of Christ Jesus Almighty he erected twelve monasteries there, into which he sent twelve monks with a superior. But he kept a few monks with him whom he judged even more ready to be instructed in his presence. At that time, noble and religious Romans also began to assemble around him and give their sons to be brought up for the service of God. Then, Euticius and the senator Tertullus delivered their promising sons, Maurus and Placid.[19] Maurus was the younger of the two boys, but since he was strong in character, he began to be his master's assistant. Placid was still a young boy.

---

19 Maurus was the son of Euticius and Placid was the son of Tertullus.

CHAPTER 4

On Returning a Wayward Monk to Salvation

In one of his monasteries that he had constructed in that place, there was a certain monk who could not stay at prayer. As soon as the brothers kneeled down to pray,[20] he would walk out and turn his mind to some earthly and transitory wanderings. After he had been frequently admonished by his abbot, he was sent up to the man of God, who also rebuked his stupidity vigorously. He followed the man of God's chastisement for barely two days after being sent back to the monastery, for on the third day he began to return to his usual custom and to wander around at the time of prayer. And when a message was sent to the servant of God by the same abbot of the monastery, he said: "I will come and correct him myself."

When the man of God came to that monastery and the brothers, after chanting the Psalms, began their prayer at the appointed hour, the man of God saw that the monk who could not remain at prayer was being dragged off by the skirt of his vestment by a dark little boy. Then he said secretly to Pompeianus, the abbot of the monastery, and to the servant of God Maurus, "Do you not see who is dragging that monk out of prayer?" They said to him, "No."

---
20 Literally, "to the study of prayer" (*ad studium orationis*).

He said to them, "Let us pray that you too may see whom the monk follows." After they had prayed for two days, Maurus saw him, but Pompeianus could not see.

So, on another day, when the man of God left the chapel after finishing his prayer, he found the monk standing outside and struck him with a rod for the blindness of his heart. From that day on, the monk did not give in to any persuasion of the dark little boy but remained still at prayer, and thus the ancient Enemy has not dared to dominate that monk's thoughts. It is as if the Devil was struck by the beating.

CHAPTER 5

On the Water Which He Produced from the Rock on Top of the Mountain

Three of the monasteries that he had established in that place were among the rocks of the mountain. It was quite laborious for the brothers to descend continually to the lake to have a drink of water, especially because of the mountain's steep slope. Those climbing down were in fear because of the danger. Then the brothers jointly went from those three monasteries to Benedict, the servant of God, saying, "It is laborious for us to descend all the way to the lake for our daily water, so it is necessary for us to move the location of our monastery." Benedict sent them away with soothing consolation, and that same night he ascended the mountain with the little boy named Placid (whom I mentioned above),[21] and he prayed there for a long time. And when he finished his prayer, he set up three stones from the place as a sign, and he returned to his monastery without the other monks knowing. When the brothers from the monasteries returned to him the next day about the necessity of their water, he said, "Go to that rock on which you will find three rocks stacked on top of each other, in a little hollow, for almighty God has the strength to produce water on the peak of

---
21 See the end of Chapter 3.

the mountain and has deigned to remove from you the labor of so great a journey." The monks went up the mountain as Benedict had told them, already beginning to sweat. When they found the place on the peak of the mountain, immediately it was full of water, which flowed out so sufficiently that even to this day it streams down abundantly from the peak to the base of the mountain.[22]

---

[22] This miracle recalls the Biblical miracle recorded in Exodus 17:1–7.

CHAPTER 6

On the Return of the Iron to the Handle from the Depths of the Water

Another time, a certain Goth[23] who was poor in spirit[24] came to the monastic way of life, and the man of God, Benedict, received him very generously. One day, he commanded that he be given an iron tool, called a *falcastrum* because it is like a pruning knife (*falx*), so that he might prune the thorn bushes in a certain place since a garden would be put there. The place the Goth undertook to clear lay next to the lake. When he cut down into the dense bushes with all his strength, the iron broke off from the handle

---

23 By calling the monk a "Goth," St. Gregory refers to his Germanic heritage. Since the Goths were traditionally pagan, we are given to understand just how foreign this monk's expected way of life would have been. Thus, St. Benedict shows how seriously he takes the responsibility to welcome all as Christ.

  It is worth noting that the Goths, led by Alaric, were responsible for the sack of Rome a century before on August 24–26, 410. The event was so startling that St. Jerome comments in a letter: "I have long wished to begin the volume of Ezekiel, and fulfil a promise frequently made to studious readers; but at the time when I had just begun to dictate the proposed exposition, my mind was so agitated by the devastation of the western provinces [of the empire], and especially of the city of Rome, that, according to the common proverb, I scarcely knew my own name; and for a long while I was silent, knowing that it is a time of tears" (*Epistle* 126, n. 2 in *Patrologiae cursus completus, Series Latina*, vol. 22 [Paris, 1845], 1086). The event also prompted St. Augustine to begin writing his monumental work *City of God*, beginning a few years after the sack.

24 See Matthew 5:3: "Blessed are the poor in spirit, for theirs is the kingdom of heaven."

On the Return of the Iron to the Handle from the Depths of the Water

and fell into the lake, which was so deep that there was no hope of retrieving the tool. Since the iron was lost, the Goth ran trembling to the monk Maurus, reported the damage he had caused, and expressed regret for his guilt. The monk Maurus went directly to the servant of God, Benedict, to tell him. Therefore, the man of the Lord, Benedict, hearing this, went to the lake, took the tool handle from the Goth's hand, and thrust it into the lake. Immediately, the iron returned from the depths and entered into the tool handle. He immediately handed the tool back to the Goth, saying: "Look! Work and be not downcast."[25]

---

25 This miracle recalls the Biblical miracle recorded in 2 Kings 6:1–7.

CHAPTER 7

On His Disciple, Who Walked Upon the Waters with His Feet

On a certain day when the same venerable Benedict was in his cell,[26] Placid, the holy man's monk, went out to draw water from the lake. Lowering his container incautiously into the lake, he fell in after it. Immediately, a wave swept him away and dragged him nearly a bowshot from shore. The man of God in his cell knew right away what had happened and called quickly to Maurus, saying, "Brother Maurus, run because that boy who went to draw water fell into the lake, and a wave has already dragged him far off!"

A marvelous thing and unknown since the apostle Peter! After asking for and receiving the blessing, moving quickly at his abbot's command, Maurus went down to the place where the boy had been swept away by the wave, ran upon the water (thinking himself to be on land), grabbed him by the hair, and quickly reversed course. As soon as he touched land, he returned to himself and looked back to where he had been.[27] Since he knew that he had run upon the waters and that he could not have anticipated doing so, he marveled and trembled with fear at what he had done. Returning to his abbot, he recounted the whole affair. And the venerable man,

---
26 That is, in his room.
27 Recall the discussion of returning to oneself in chapter 3.

28

Benedict, did not attribute it to his merits but to his obedience. But Maurus, on the contrary, said that he did it only because of Benedict's command and that he was conscious that he did not have within him the power to do it and he did not know he was doing it at the time. But in this friendly contention of mutual humility,[28] the boy who was pulled out of the water made the determination as an eyewitness. For he said, "When I was being dragged away by the water, I saw the abbot's garment upon my head, and I thought that it drew me forth from the waters."[29]

PETER: These are great things that you narrate and beneficial for the building up of many. The more I drink of the miracles of the good man, the more I thirst to hear more.

---

28 See *The Rule of St. Benedict,* chapter 72: "They should each try to be the first to show respect to the other."
29 This miracle recalls the Biblical miracle recorded in Matthew 14:22–33.

CHAPTER 8

Of the Poisoned Bread Carried Far Off by the Raven

~~~~

GREGORY: When the people in that place grew fervent in love of Our Lord God Jesus Christ and knowledge of this fervor spread abroad, many people gave up their worldly life and tamed the neck of their heart under the easy yoke of the Redeemer.[30] Then, as it is characteristic of the depraved to envy the good for their virtue despite not desiring to have that virtue for themselves, a priest of the neighboring church named Florentius, grandfather of our subdeacon Florentius, was assaulted by the ancient Enemy's wickedness and began to be envious of the holy man's virtue, to disparage his way of life, and even to stop as many people as he could from visiting Benedict.

He saw that he could not hinder Benedict's holy progress, his way of life's increasingly favorable opinion, or his success incessantly calling many people to a better state of life. Upon realizing all this, Florentius became a worse man, inflamed by the torches of increased envy. He desired the praise that comes from having Benedict's way of life, but he did not wish to have that praiseworthy life. He was blinded by the darkness of his envy to the point that he poisoned a loaf of bread and sent it to the servant of the Lord

---
30 See Matthew 11:30.

Almighty as if it were a present. The man of God received the bread with gratitude, but it was not hidden from him that a curse lay hidden in the bread.

A raven would typically come from a nearby forest at Benedict's mealtime and take bread from his hand. When the raven had come as usual, the man of God threw the bread that the priest had sent over to the raven and instructed it, saying, "In the name of the Lord Jesus Christ, take this bread and throw it away in a place where no man could possibly find it." Then the raven, with open mouth and extended wings, began to run circles around the bread and caw, as if it were saying publicly that it wanted to obey, but it could not fulfill the command. The man of God directed the bird repeatedly, saying, "Take up the bread! Take it up without fear and throw it where it could not be found." After some delay, the raven took up the loaf, rose, and flew off. Three hours later it returned without the bread and took its customary daily provision from the man of God's hand. But the venerable abbot, seeing that the priest's mind burned against his life, grieved more for him than for himself.[31]

But the aforementioned Florentius, since he could not kill the master's body, burned to extinguish the souls of his disciples, such that he sent seven naked young women into the garden of the monastery where Benedict lived. The women joined hands and danced for a time in order that they might inflame their minds to the perversity of lust. When the holy man saw this affair from the monastery, he immediately feared for his younger disciples. And thinking that they were sent for his persecution alone, he gave way to Florentius' envy. He set in order all the monasteries he had established, with their brothers under their superiors, and he moved his home, taking only a few monks with him.

---

31 This episode recalls the Biblical events recounted in 1 Kings 17:1–7.

As soon as the man of God humbly gave way to his hatred, almighty God struck Florentius terribly. For when the priest, standing on the balcony, knew and rejoiced that Benedict had departed, the balcony on which he was standing fell, though the rest of the house remained unmoved, and killed Florentius, crushing the enemy of Benedict. Maurus, the man of God's disciple, knowing what had happened, immediately reported to venerable Abbot Benedict, who was hardly ten miles away from the place, saying, "Come back because the priest who was persecuting you is dead." When Benedict, the man of God, heard this news, he lamented gravely both because his enemy had died and because his disciple rejoiced in the death of his enemy. For this reason, he announced a penance for his disciple because he presumed to encourage such joy at the death of the enemy.[32]

PETER: The things you say are amazing and greatly astounding. For I see Moses in the water produced from the stone, Elisha in the iron drawn back from the depths of the water, Peter in the journey upon the water, Elijah in the obedience of the raven, David in the lament at the death of an enemy.[33] And I think that this man was full of the spirit of all the just.

GREGORY: Peter, the man of God, Benedict, had the spirit of the One who filled the hearts of all the elect with the imparted grace of redemption, about whom John said, "He was the true light which illuminates all men coming into this world."[34] And about whom it is also written, "And from his fullness we have all received."[35] For God's holy men could have powers from the Lord but not pass them on to others. And he, who promised he was going to give the

---

32 This episode recalls the Biblical events recounted in 2 Samuel 1:11–12.
33 See Exodus 17:1–7; 2 Kings 6:1–7; Matthew 14:22–33; 1 Kings 17:1–7; and 2 Samuel 1:11–12.
34 See John 1:9.
35 See John 1:16.

sign of Jonah to his enemies,[36] gave signs of power to his subjects such that he deigned to die in the sight of the proud and to rise in the sight of the humble. He did all this so that they may see what he condemned and what they ought to love and worship. By this mystery, it happens that while the proud see the despicableness of his death, the humble receive the glory of his power against death.

PETER: I now ask you where the holy man went, or if he later showed any miracles there openly.

GREGORY: The holy man changed his place, but he did not change his enemy. For the more he endured serious battles, the more he found the very master of wickedness fighting against him openly. His fortress, which is called Cassino, lies hidden on the side of a high mountain, which mountain receives the fortress on a broad ledge.[37] But the mountain rises three miles higher above the fortress as if stretching its peak to the heavens, where there was a very ancient temple where Apollo was worshipped by the foolish countryfolk in the custom of the ancient Gentiles. All around this temple, a grove of trees grew up for the worship of demons, and even at that time the unfaithful stained them with a great number of insane sacrilegious sacrifices. Therefore, arriving there, the man of God crushed the idol, overturned the altar, and cut down the woods. He built the chapel of St. Martin in the very temple of Apollo, but where the altar of the same Apollo was, he constructed a chapel of St. John and called the multitude, who were lingering around, to faith by continual preaching.

But this ancient Enemy, not bearing this silently, showed himself openly before the eyes of the abbot by an apparition, not hiddenly nor through sleep. He complained about the violence he suffered with such great cries that the brothers also heard his voice, although they did not see him. As the venerable abbot said to his disciples,

---
36 See Matthew 16:4.
37 Notice the description of the monastery as a fortress.

the most disgraceful and inflamed ancient Enemy appeared to his bodily eyes and seemed to rage at him with flaming mouth and eyes. What the Devil said to Benedict, all the monks heard. For first he called him by name, and when the man of God did not answer, he erupted indignantly at his character. For when he called out, saying, "Benedict! Benedict!" and saw Benedict not responding to him at all, he immediately added, "Cursed, and not Blessed,[38] what have you to do with me? Why do you persecute me?" But now we will examine the ancient Enemy's new battles against the servant of God, against whom he willingly fought, but against his will he provided Benedict many occasions of victory.

---

[38] There is a play on words here. Recall that Benedict's name (*Benedictus*) means blessed. When Benedict does not respond to his name, "Blessed! Blessed!" ("*Benedictus!*"), Satan turns and calls him by the opposite name, "Cursed" (*Maledictus*).

CHAPTER 9

On the Removal of a Large Stone Through His Prayer

One day when the brothers were building the rooms of the monastery, a stone lay among them that they had decided to use for the building. When two or three monks could not move it, many monks were added, but still it remained unmovable, as if it were stuck fast in the earth by the roots. They were able to understand plainly that the ancient Enemy himself had sat upon it, which the hands of so many men could not move. Since they were faced with this difficulty, word was sent to the man of God that he might come and drive off the Enemy by his praying so that the stone could be moved. Benedict immediately came and gave a blessing with prayer. And the stone was lifted with such speed that it was as if it had none of its prior weight.

CHAPTER 10

On the Imaginary Flame in the Kitchen

Then, it was pleasing in the sight of the man of God that they should dig where the stone had been. When they had dug down deep, the brothers found a bronze idol. They threw it by chance into the kitchen for a time, where they suddenly saw a fire spring up, and in the eyes of all the monks the entire kitchen was consumed in the blaze. Because they caused a great commotion and noise throwing water on the fire to extinguish it, the man of God came, drawn by the uproar. Seeing that the brothers saw fire and not seeing any fire with his own eyes, he immediately bowed his head in prayer. And he called those brothers, whom he found deluded by the imaginary fire, to see what he saw so that they might recognize that the kitchen building was safe and so that they might not see the flames, which the ancient Enemy had produced in their minds.

CHAPTER 11

On the Crushed and Healed Little Servant of God

Again, the man of God stayed behind in prayer[39] in his room while the brothers built the wall, since it needed to be raised a little higher. The ancient Enemy appeared to him in an insulting manner and indicated that he would go to the laboring brothers. The man of God swiftly showed this plan to the brothers, saying, "Brothers, caution! Come here because an evil spirit comes to you right at this moment!" The man who had passed along the order barely got the words out when the evil spirit threw down that wall that was being built. And one monk, who was a little boy, the son of a senator, was crushed by the destruction. All the brothers were saddened and sorely afflicted, not for the ruined wall, but with grief for the brother. They immediately set off with great sorrow to tell venerable Abbot Benedict.

Then, the same abbot ordered that the boy, who was crushed to pieces, be brought to him. They were only able to carry him in a cloak because the collapsed stones of the wall had crushed not only his limbs but even his bones. The man of God immediately ordered him to be placed in his room on the mat (*spytathio*) on which he was accustomed to pray. He sent the brothers out of the

---
39 Literally, "in the study of prayer" (*in orationis studio*).

room and closed the door. He lay prostrate in prayer more intently than usual. A miraculous thing! At that very hour he sent this boy, healed and as strong as ever, back to the same labor, so that he might finish the wall with the brothers.[40] The ancient Enemy had believed he could insult Benedict by his death. But the man of God began to abound in a spirit of prophecy to preach things to come and to announce absent things to those present.

---

40 This episode recalls the Biblical events recounted in 2 Kings 4:32–37.

CHAPTER 12

On the Monks Who Ate Outside the Kitchen

It was the custom of the monastery that whenever the brothers went out on some business, they ate no food and drink outside the monastery.[41] This part of the rule was carefully observed. One day brothers were sent out on business, in which they were detained longer than expected. As a result, they stayed with a pious woman they knew, in whose house they ate some food. When they returned late to the monastery, they asked the blessing of the abbot as is the custom. He promptly delayed the blessing, saying, "Where did you eat?" They answered him, saying, "Nowhere." He said to them, "Why are you lying? Did you not enter the house of such a woman? Did you not eat these and those foods? Did you not drink such drinks?"[42] When the venerable abbot had told them the house of the woman, the kinds of food, and the number of drinks, they fell trembling at his feet, recognizing together what they had done, and they confessed their failure. But he immediately pardoned their guilt, weighing the fact that they would not act otherwise

---
41 See *The Rule of St. Benedict*, chapter 51:1: "If a brother is sent on some errand and expects to return to the monastery that same day, he must not presume to eat outside, even if he receives a pressing invitation."
42 The implication from St. Gregory's words here is that St. Benedict is recounting the exact woman and the exact foods and drinks they had, even though they had not told him.

in his absence because they would know he was present to them in spirit.

CHAPTER 13

On the Brother of Valentinian Who Also Ate Outside the Kitchen

Again, the brother of Benedict's monk Valentinian, whom we mentioned at the beginning, was a layman, but devout.[43] He was accustomed to come fasting to the monastery each year to learn the prayer of the servant of God and to see his brother. One day while he made his journey to the monastery, another traveler joined with him who carried food for himself on the journey. Since the hour had already grown late, he said, "Come, brother, let us eat the food, lest we be exhausted on the way." The brother of Valentinian answered him, "God forbid, brother! I will not do it because I always go to Abbot Benedict fasting." His fellow traveler fell silent at that response. But a bit later, when they had gone a short distance on the journey, the traveler again suggested that they eat. The brother, who had decided to arrive fasting, refused to consent. Then the man who invited him to eat was silent and agreed to travel a little further with him fasting.

When they had gone a long way on the journey and walking at such a late hour wearied them, they came on the journey to a

---
43 See the Preface.

meadow, spring, and whatever else could seem pleasurable for refreshing the body. Then the fellow traveler said, "Look, water! Look, a meadow! Look, a beautiful place in which we could be refreshed and rest a little. We would be strong to finish our journey unharmed." Therefore, when the words coaxed his ears and the place his eyes, he consented to this third suggestion and ate.[44] He arrived at the monastery in the evening. And, presented to venerable Abbot Benedict, he asked for his prayer. But right away the holy man reproached the thing he had done on the way, saying, "Brother, what did the wicked Enemy, who was your fellow traveler, say to you? He could not persuade you the first time. He could not the second time. He persuaded you the third time, and he got what he wanted: to defeat you." Then the man acknowledged the guilt of his weak mind, prostrated himself at Abbot Benedict's feet, and began to cry and blush all the more at his guilt knowing that he had failed in the eyes of Abbot Benedict, although he had been absent.

PETER: I see the spirit of Elijah present in the breast of the holy man, who was present to his absent disciples.[45]

GREGORY: Peter, you must be silent a while so that you may know more.

---

44 This description echoes the words of the Bible in Genesis 3:6.
45 See 2 Kings 1:2–4.

CHAPTER 14

On Catching King Totila's Subterfuge

For in the time of the Goths when Totila,[46] their king, heard that the holy man had the gift of prophecy, he traveled to his monastery, stopped a little way off, and announced his coming to Benedict. A command promptly was sent forth from the monastery that he might come. As he had a faithless heart, he tried to discover whether the man of God had the spirit of prophecy. He provided his boots to one of his guards named Ricchus, clothed him in the royal garments, and instructed the guard to go up to the man of God as if Ricchus were the king. He sent three men in his retinue who were accustomed to attend to the king before the others, namely, Wilderich and Blidin,[47] so that they might enter before the eyes of the servant of God and so conceal that the man was pretending to be the king Totila. He also offered other attendants and guards so that Benedict might think he was the king as much because of the servants as because of the purple robes. When Ricchus, clothed in the robes, had entered the monastery accompanied by such a

---

46 Totila was king of the Ostrogoths from 541–552. He was elected king after arranging the assassination of his predecessor. Totila reconquered almost all of the Italian territories that the Eastern Roman Empire had taken in 540. As St. Benedict prophesied, Totila would capture Rome and then go on to Sicily.

47 Older versions of *The Life and Miracles of St. Benedict* list the names "Vuld, Ruderic, and Blidin."

great crowd of attendants, the man of God sat afar off. Once they had come close enough that they could hear him, Benedict cried out, saying, "Take off those clothes, son. Take off all you wear, for it is not yours." Ricchus immediately fell to the ground, and he became frightened because he had presumed to trick such a man. All those who had come with him to the man of God fell to the ground, too. And rising back up, they did not dare to approach him, but they returned to the king and reported their fear in having been caught with such force.

CHAPTER 15

On the Prophecy Made About King Totila

Then Totila himself came to the man of God. When he saw Benedict sitting afar off, he did not dare to approach and threw himself onto the ground. The man of God said to him, "Arise," but he did not dare to rise from the ground before him. Then Benedict, the servant of Jesus Christ, himself deigned to approach the prostrate king, raised him from the earth, and rebuked his actions. He prophesied tersely all the things that were going to happen to him, saying, "You do many wicked things. You have done many wicked things. Give up your iniquity already! Indeed, you are going to enter Rome, cross the sea, reign for nine years, and die in the tenth." Upon hearing these things, the king returned to the ground begging vehemently in prayer, and he was less cruel from that time on. When he went to Rome not long after, he passed on to Sicily. But in the tenth year of his reign, by the judgment of God Almighty, he lost his reign together with his life.

Moreover, the bishop of the Church of Canusa was accustomed to come to the servant of the Lord. The man of God loved this bishop greatly because of the merit of his life. Thus, when he had conferred with him about the coming of King Totila and the destruction of the Roman city, he said, "This city was destroyed through this king so that it might not be inhabited any longer." The man of God answered him, "Rome will not be exterminated by foreign nations but by violent storms and whirlwinds, and, wearied by the motion of the earth, it will wither of itself." The prophetic mystery of this claim has already appeared to us in a clearer light. We find in this city walls destroyed, houses overturned, churches destroyed by the whirlwind, and her edifices wearied by long gloom because we see that they are laid low by widespread destruction. Although Honoratus, his disciple, who related the story to me, did not hear it from Benedict's mouth himself, he heard it from the brothers.

CHAPTER 16

On the Cleric Liberated from a Demon

At the same time, a cleric of the church of Aquino was harassed by a demon. The venerable bishop of his church, Constantine, had sent him to many martyrs' shrines so that he could be healed. But the martyred saints of God did not will to grant the gift of health, so that they might demonstrate how much grace was in Benedict. Thus, the cleric was led to Benedict, the servant of Almighty God, who, pouring out prayers to Christ Jesus, the Lord, immediately expelled the ancient Enemy from the possessed man. He instructed the healed man, saying: "Go, and do not eat meat after this, and never presume to advance to Holy Orders.[48] On whatever day you presume to violate this sacred order, you will immediately surrender your right to the Devil again." So the healed cleric departed, and since recent punishments usually terrify the mind, he observed for a while those things that the man of God instructed. But when many years later all his superiors passed on from this life and he saw those below him elevated above him in Holy Orders, he disregarded the words of the man of God as if they were forgotten because they were far past. He received Holy

---

48 Since the Second Vatican Council, the clerical state has been restricted to bishops, priests, and deacons, that is, those who have received the sacrament of Holy Orders. In St. Benedict's time, some men who were not yet ordained were also considered clerics.

Orders, and immediately the Devil, who had relinquished him, caught hold of him and harassed him, and he did not cease until he drove him out of his mind.

PETER: This man of God, as it seems to me, even penetrated hidden things of divinity, since he saw that this cleric would be handed over to the Devil unless he did not dare accept Holy Orders.

GREGORY: Why should a man who serves the commands of divinity not know the secret things of divinity, when it is written, "He who clings to the Lord is one spirit with him"?[49]

PETER: If he who clings to the Lord becomes one spirit with the Lord, why does the same excellent preacher also say, "Who knows the mind of the Lord, or who was his counselor?"[50] For it seems to be most unfitting not to know his mind when he is made one with him.

GREGORY: Holy men are not ignorant of the Lord's mind insofar as they are one with the Lord. For the same apostle Paul also says, "For which men know the things that are of man except the spirit of man that is in him? So too no one knows the things that are of God except the spirit of God."[51] To show that he knows the things of God, he added, "But we have not received the spirit of this world, but the Spirit who is from God."[52] Again, it is said in the same place, "Eye has not seen nor ear heard, nor has it arisen in the heart of man, what God has prepared for those who love him, but he has revealed it to us through his Spirit."[53]

PETER: So, if those things that are of God have been revealed to the apostle Paul through the Spirit of God, what does it mean when

---
49 See 1 Corinthians 6:17.
50 See Romans 11:34.
51 See 1 Corinthians 2:11.
52 See 1 Corinthians 2:12.
53 See 1 Corinthians 2:9–10.

he said, "O the depth of the riches of wisdom and knowledge of God! How incomprehensible are his judgments and unsearchable his ways!"[54] But a question about these other sayings arises in me again. For David the prophet speaks to the Lord, saying, "With my lips I have pronounced all the judgments of your mouth."[55] And since it is less to know than to pronounce, why is it that Paul asserts the judgments of God to be incomprehensible, but David testifies not only to know them all but even to have pronounced them with his lips?

GREGORY: I have answered both of these for you briefly above when I said that holy men, insofar as they are one with God, are not ignorant of the Lord's mind. For all who devoutly follow the Lord are with God in devotion, but carrying the weight of corruptible flesh, they are not with God yet. Thus, they know the hidden judgments of God insofar as they are joined to him, and they do not know the hidden judgments of God insofar as they are not joined to him. For since they do not now penetrate his secrets perfectly, they give witness that his judgments are incomprehensible. But those who cling with their minds recognize, know, and proclaim either the eloquences of Sacred Scripture or hidden revelations insofar as they receive them by clinging to God. Therefore, they do not know the judgments that God keeps silent, and they do know the judgments that God speaks. Consequently, the prophet David, when he says, "With my lips I have pronounced all judgments," immediately added "from your mouth," as if to declare openly: I have been able to know and pronounce those judgments that I have known you to have spoken.[56] For without a doubt you have hidden those things from our thoughts that you do not speak to him. Therefore, the prophetic and apostolic judgments are harmonized because God's judgments are incomprehensible.

---

54 Romans 11:33.
55 Psalm 119:13.
56 Psalm 119:13.

And yet the things that have been uttered from his mouth are pronounced by human lips since they can be known by men and uttered through God and they cannot be hidden.

PETER: That response clearly answers the objection of my little question. But I ask you to add anything else that might be said of this man's virtue.

CHAPTER 17

On the Prophecy of His Monastery's Destruction

GREGORY: A certain nobleman named Theopropus was converted by the warning of Abbot Benedict and shared great confidence and friendship with Benedict for the merit of his life. One day, when Theopropus had entered Benedict's cell, he found Benedict crying most bitterly. Standing there a long while, he saw that his tears would not stop. The man of God was accustomed to mourning in prayer but not to wailing, so Theopropus asked what was the cause of such great lamentation. The man of God answered him, "This whole monastery, which I have built and prepared together with the brothers, is going to be handed over to the nations by God Almighty's judgment. But I could barely obtain that the souls in this place would be saved." Theopropus heard his voice, but we certify and know that his monastery is now destroyed by the Langobards. For not long ago, the Langobards entered at night when the brothers were resting and tore the whole place apart, but they could not lay hold of even one man there. Almighty God fulfilled what he had promised to his faithful servant Benedict, that if he handed the monastery over to the nations, he would guard the souls. In this affair I see Benedict holding the place of Paul, who, although his ship had suffered the loss of all their supplies, received the life of all those who were commended to him as consolation.[57]

---

[57] See Acts 27:13–24.

CHAPTER 18

On the Flagon Cast Off and Known through the Spirit

One time our Exhilaratus, whom you know well, was sent by his master to the man of God with two little wooden vessels that are commonly known as flagons. He took one to the monastery, but he hid the other as he walked on his journey. And the man of the Lord, from whom deeds done elsewhere could not be hidden, received one with thanksgiving and, stooping, warned the boy, saying: "See, son, that you do not drink from that flagon you have hidden. Turn it upside down and find what is in it." He went forth from the man of God greatly confused, and he went back wanting to test what he had heard. When he turned the flagon upside down, a serpent immediately came out of it. Then the boy Exhilaratus became frightened at the evil he had done because of what he found in the wine.

CHAPTER 19

On the Napkins Received by the Servant of God

There was a village not far from the monastery in which a great multitude of men were converted from idolatry to faith in God by Benedict's exhortation. In that place there were also some holy nuns, and the servant of God, Benedict, cared for their souls by sending his brothers to them for encouragement. Now one day he sent a monk, as was his custom, but the monk he had sent, after he had made his admonition, took some napkins at the request of the religious women, and he hid them in his breast pocket. As soon as he had returned, the man of God began to rebuke him with great sharpness, saying: "Why has iniquity entered into your breast?" But he was stupefied and, forgetting what he had done, did not know why he was being rebuked. Benedict said to him, "Was I not present there when you took the napkins from the handmaidens of the Lord and put them in your breast pocket?" The monk immediately repented of having acted so foolishly, prostrated himself at Benedict's feet, and threw away the napkins that he had hidden in his breast pocket.

CHAPTER 20

On the Knowledge of an Arrogant Boy Known Through the Spirit

Another day, while the venerable Abbot Benedict was taking bodily nourishment late in the evening, his monk, who was the son of a lawyer, was holding a candle by the table for him. As the man of God ate, the monk stood in his ministry with the candle. Through a spirit of arrogance, this silent monk began to turn things over in his mind and think to himself, "Who is he whom *I* assist in his eating, holding the candle and devoting service? Who am *I* that I should serve him?"[58] The man of God turned to him and began to rebuke him sharply, saying: "Sign your heart, Brother! What is it that you say? Sign your heart." He immediately instructed the assembled brothers, took the candle from his hands, and commanded him to withdraw from the ministry and sit quietly by him for the rest of dinner. Asked later by the brothers what was in his heart, he told them how he was swollen with the spirit of pride and what words he had said hiddenly in his thoughts against the man of God. Then it was clear to all that nothing could be hidden from venerable Benedict, in whose ears rang even the words of thoughts.

---

58 In Latin, the pronoun "I" (*ego*) is not often used because "I" is included in the meaning of the Latin verb. Here, however, St. Gregory includes *ego* to emphasize the pride in the monk's thoughts.

CHAPTER 21

On the Two Hundred Measures of Flour Found Outside His Cell in Time of Famine

Another time in the same region of Campania, a famine began, and a great lack of food set in. There was already a lack of wheat in Benedict's monastery, and even the bread was consumed so that no more than five loaves could be found for the brothers to eat. When the venerable Abbot saw that they were discouraged, he directed their faintheartedness to straighten up with a mild reproof and to rise up again with a promise, saying, "Why is your heart saddened from a lack of bread? Indeed, today there is less, but tomorrow you will have bread abundantly." And on the following day, they found two hundred measures of flour in sacks outside the door of his cell. No one knows by whom Almighty God had sent it. When the brothers saw this, they gave thanks to the Lord and were taught not to be doubtful about abundance in extreme poverty.

PETER: Tell me, I ask you, is it possible to believe that the spirit of prophecy could always be with this servant of God? Or did the spirit of prophecy fill his mind from time to time?

GREGORY: Peter, the spirit of prophecy does not always shine forth in the minds of the prophets because, just as John wrote of the Holy Spirit, "He blows where he wills,"[59] so too you should know that he blows when he wants. For there is the example of Nathan; asked by the king if he could construct the temple, he first consented and then prohibited him.[60] There is the example of Elijah; not knowing the reason why the woman was crying, he said to the boy to prohibit her: "Send her away because her soul is in bitter distress, and the Lord hides the reason from me and does not show it to me."[61] Because Almighty God disposes things by the disposition of his great piety, when he gives the spirit of prophecy at some time and takes it away at another time, he both elevates the minds of the prophets in the heights and guards them in humility so that, accepting the spirit, they may discover what things are from God and further know what things are from themselves when they do not have the spirit of prophecy.

PETER: Your strong reasoning cries out that it is as you say it is. But I ask you to continue explaining whatever you remember happening to the venerable Abbot Benedict.

---

59 See John 3:8.
60 See 2 Samuel 7:1–17.
61 See 2 Kings 4:27.

CHAPTER 22

On the Vision by Which He Commanded the Building of the Monastery in Terracina

GREGORY: Another time, he was invited by a certain faithful man so that he might be obliged to send his disciples to the man's farm near the city of Terracina to build a monastery. Consenting to the man, he sent some monks and established an abbot and prior. He promised those who were going, saying, "Go, and on that day, I will come and show you where you ought to build the chapel, the dining hall, the guest house, and whatever else is necessary." After they obtained his blessing, they immediately went out, and waiting anxiously for the established day, they prepared all the things that seemed necessary to them for his arrival. On the night before the promised day, the man of the Lord appeared in a dream to the servant of God whom Abbot Benedict made abbot and to the prior. He designated in detail the location where they ought to build what. When the abbot and prior arose from sleep, they related to each other what they had seen. Nevertheless, not giving full faith to that vision, they watched for the man of God as he promised to come.

When the man of God did not come on the established day, they returned to him in grief, saying, "We expected you to come,

Father Abbot, like you promised, and you would show us where we ought to build, but you did not come." He answered them, "Why, brothers? Why do you say these things? Did I not come as I promised?" They replied, "When did you come?" He answered, "Did I not appear to each of you as you were sleeping and designate each place? Go, and build every bit of the monastery as you heard in the vision." Hearing these things and wondering at them greatly, they returned to the farm and constructed all the buildings as they had learned from the revelation.

PETER: I wish to be taught how he could give his response to them as they were sleeping afar off and how they heard and recognized him through the vision.

GREGORY: Why is it that you desire to investigate the order of these events, Peter? It is obvious that the nature of the spirit is more mobile than the nature of the body. And we know with certainty by the witness of Scripture that a prophet was suddenly lifted up out of Judea and set down in Chaldea with his midday meal, and after he refreshed another prophet with the meal, he suddenly found himself in Judea again.[62] Therefore, if Habakkuk could go so far bodily in a moment carrying his meal, what wonder is it if Abbot Benedict went so far in spirit and told the necessary things to the spirits of the resting brothers? Just as Habakkuk went bodily for the food of the body, so too Benedict travelled spiritually for the institution of spiritual life.

PETER: I confess that the hand of your speech wipes away the doubt of my mind. But I want to know what sort of man he was in his common conversations.

---

62 Daniel 14:33–39.

CHAPTER 23

On the Handmaidens of God Who Returned to Communion After Their Death by His Offering

~~~~~~

GREGORY: None of his ordinary speech was lacking the weight of virtue, Peter, since he placed his heart in the heights. No words fell from his mouth in vain. If ever he spoke something not in a discerning manner but in a threatening manner, his word had so much power that it was as if his speech was pronounced in judgment and was not doubtful or uncertain. For not far from his monastery, two religious women of noble birth lived in their own home, and a certain religious man served all their external needs. But just as nobility of birth often breeds ignobility of mind in some, so those who remember their own status more than other things do not humble themselves in this world. Similarly, these religious women had not yet restrained their tongues under a religious habit, and they provoked the religious man who provided for all their external necessities to resentment by their frequently incautious speech. When the man had put up with this speech for some time, he went to the man of God and told him how much he suffered the abuse of their words. And the man of God, hearing about these things, immediately ordered the religious women, saying, "Correct your tongues, because if you do not mend your ways, I will excommunicate you." He inflicted this judgment of excommunication not by pronouncing it but by threatening it.

Those religious women did not change from their former ways. After a few days, they died and were buried in the church. When a solemn Mass was celebrated in the same church, the deacon, as is his custom, cried out, "If anyone is not in communion with the Church, let him leave this place." The religious women's nurse, who was accustomed to make offerings for them to the Lord, saw them rise from their graves and leave the church. She often perceived this happen. They went outside at the voice of the deacon crying out, and they could not remain in the church. She remembered what the man of God commanded them while they were still alive. (He, of course, said that he would deprive them of communion unless they corrected their words and character.) Then, she told the servant of God what she had seen with grave sorrow, and he immediately gave the offering to her with his own hand, saying, "Go, and offer this offering to the Lord for them, and they will no longer be excommunicated."

PETER: How amazing! Although this man was venerable and holy, while still in this corruptible flesh he could unbind souls already standing in the invisible trial.

GREGORY: Not at all, Peter. Was not the man who heard these words also in this flesh: "Whatever you shall bind on earth will be bound also in heaven, and whatever you loose on earth will also be loosed in heaven"?[63] Those who hold the place of holy authority in faith and morals obtain now the same binding and loosing. But in order that man may be so great on earth, the Maker of heaven and earth came from heaven to earth, and in order that he could

---

63 See Matthew 16:19. Christ spoke these words to St. Peter.

judge spiritual matters in the flesh and give to man abundantly, he deigned to become God in the flesh for men. Consequently, since he gathered our infirmity upon himself, the strength of God undergirds our infirmity.

PETER: Your reasoning is in harmony with the strength of his miracles.

CHAPTER 24

Of the Young Monk Whom the Earth Cast from His Grave

GREGORY: Again, on a certain day one of his very young monks, who loved his parents more than he ought, went out of the monastery to their house without Benedict's blessing. He died immediately as soon as he came to them, on the same day. When he was buried, his body was found thrown outside the next day. They took care to bury him again, but the following day, his body was found exhumed outside as before. Then, running quickly to Abbot Benedict, they threw themselves at his feet with great weeping, that he might deign to bestow abundantly his aid upon the boy. The man of God immediately gave them Communion of the Lord's Body by his own hand, saying, "Go and place the Lord's Body upon the boy's breast with great reverence, and bury him like that." When they had done this, the earth received and held his body. It was not thrown out of the tomb again.

Weigh carefully, Peter, the merits of this man in the eyes of the Lord Jesus Christ, that even the earth rejected his body whom Benedict had not blessed.

PETER: I weigh them clearly, and I am stupefied.

CHAPTER 25

On the Monk Who Found a Dragon Against Him on the Way

GREGORY: There was a monk given to mental mobility, and he did not want to stay in the monastery. The man of God corrected him regularly and admonished him frequently, but he in no way consented to persist in the community, and he begged earnestly to be released from his vows. One day, the venerable Abbot, irritated by the nuisance of his excessive complaining, ordered him to go. Immediately when he departed from the monastery, he found a dragon standing on the way facing him with open mouth. Since the dragon that had appeared wanted to devour him, the monk began to cry out in a loud voice, trembling and quivering: "Run! Run! This dragon is going to devour me!" But the brothers, running out to him, saw no dragon, and they led the trembling and palpitating monk back into the monastery. The monk immediately promised never to leave the monastery and remained in his vows from that hour. Of course, by the prayers of the holy man he saw the dragon, whom he had followed before without seeing it, standing in opposition to him.

CHAPTER 26

On the Boy Cured of Leprosy

~~~~~~

But I think I should not pass over in silence what I know of a brilliant man named Anthony, whose father's servant was afflicted with leprosy such that his hair had already fallen out and his skin had swollen. He could no longer hide the increasing pus. Anthony sent the boy from his father to the man of God, who restored him to his prior health with all swiftness.

CHAPTER 27

On the Gold Coins Returned to a Debtor Through a Miracle

~~~~~~

Nor will I hide what his disciple, Peregrine, used to tell. One day, a certain faithful man driven by the necessity of debt believed that the only remedy open to him was if he traveled to the man of God and related the necessity of debt that pressed down upon him. Thus, he came to the monastery, found the servant of Almighty God, and recounted how he was sorely afflicted by his creditor for twelve gold coins. The venerable abbot answered the man that he had never had twelve coins, but he still consoled the man in his poverty with pleasant speech, saying: "Go, and return after two days. I do not have it to give to you today." For the next two days, he was taken up with prayer, as was his custom. When the man who was afflicted by the necessity of debt returned on the third day, they immediately found thirteen gold coins on the monastery's chest, which was full of wheat. The man of God ordered the coins to be carried out and given to the afflicted beggar, saying that he should return twelve for the debt and have one for his own expenses.

But I now return to those things that I know of his disciples, of whom I spoke earlier in the book. A certain man carried on a very serious rivalry with his enemy, whose hatred surged up even to the point that he gave the unsuspecting man poison to drink. Although the poison was not strong enough to destroy his life, still it changed the color of his skin so that the diverse variety of colors on his body seemed to imitate leprosy. But, led before the servant of God, he received the original health of his skin, for immediately, as Benedict touched him, all the variety of colors of his skin took flight.

CHAPTER 28

On the Glass Bottle Thrown Against the Rock and Not Broken

At that time when a lack of food greatly afflicted Campania, the man of God distributed all the goods of his monastery to the needy so that nothing remained in the cellar except a little bit of oil in a glass vessel.[64] Then, a certain subdeacon named Agapitus arrived, earnestly asking that he should be given a little oil. The man of the Lord, who resolved to give away all things on earth so that he might reserve all things in heaven, ordered the little bit of oil that remained to be given to the man. But the monk who was the cellarer heard the words of the command yet was reluctant to fulfill them.[65]

After a little while, Benedict inquired if the monk had given what he was commanded, and the monk answered that he had not given it because if he had made that present, absolutely nothing would be left for the brothers. Then, in anger Benedict instructed the others to take the glass vessel in which the little oil remained and throw it out the window, lest anything remain in the cellar

---
64 See Chapter 21 for the earlier account of famine in Campania.
65 See *The Rule of St. Benedict* chapter 31 for the description of the monastery "cellarer," who provided the food for the community.

through disobedience. So it was done. Under that window there was a steep hill with a heap of sharp rocks at the bottom. The glass vessel that had been thrown fell to the rocks, but it remained unharmed, as if it had never been thrown, so that it could neither be broken nor the oil spilled. The man of the Lord commanded it to be retrieved and to be given to the one who had asked for it. Then, gathering the brothers, he rebuked the disobedient monk in their presence for his infidelity and pride.

CHAPTER 29

On the Large Jug Emptied and Filled with Oil

After he had completed his reproof, he gave himself over to prayer with the brothers. But in the same place where he was praying with the brothers, there was an empty, covered oil jug. When the holy man persisted in prayer, the lid began to be raised by the increasing oil in the jug. The oil spilled over the jug's brim and flooded the floor. When the servant of God, Benedict, beheld this, he completed his prayer at once, and the flow of oil upon the floor ceased.

Then, he extensively admonished the distrustful and disobedient brother so that he might learn to have faith and humility. And the same brother, healthily corrected, blushed for shame since the venerable abbot showed the power of the Lord Almighty by admonition and miracles. Nor could anyone later doubt any of his promises, who all in a moment had restored the empty glass jar full of oil.

CHAPTER 30

On a Monk Liberated from a Demon

On a certain day when he traveled to the chapel of St. John, which is on the very summit of a mountain, the ancient Enemy came against him in the appearance of a physician on a mule and carrying a horn and a pestle.[66] When Benedict hailed the physician, saying, "Where are you going?" he answered, "Behold, I go to the brothers to give them a potion." And so venerable Benedict continued to the chapel and returned in haste when he had finished praying. But the malign spirit found one of the senior monks drinking water. He immediately entered into the monk, threw him to the ground, and harassed him terribly. When the man of God, returning from prayer, saw him cruelly harassed, he gave him just a blow upon the cheek. Immediately, he cast the malign spirit from him so that he would not dare return to him again.

PETER: I want to know if he always obtained such great miracles by the power of prayer or if he sometimes produced them at the mere command of his will.

GREGORY: Those who cling to God with a devout mind can exhibit miracles in either way when necessity demands it. Sometimes miraculous things happen from prayer, sometimes from power. As

---
66 See chapter 8 for the account of the construction of the chapel of St. John.

John says, "However many received him, he gave them the power to become sons of God."[67] Because if the sons of God are from power, what wonder is it that they are strong enough to work miracles from power? St. Peter gives witness that they produce miracles in each way, for he revived Tabitha from death by prayer, and he handed Ananias and Sapphira over to death by his rebuke.[68] For we do not read that he prayed in the case of their death, but only that he rebuked the offense that they committed. It is confirmed, therefore, that sometimes they produce these miracles from power and sometimes from petition, given that he took away their life by rebuking and restored hers by praying. Now I will also recount two deeds of the faithful servant of God, Benedict, in which it shines clearly that he received some things divinely from power and he could do others from prayer.

---

67 See John 1:12.
68 See Acts 9:40 and 5:1–11.

CHAPTER 31

On the Bound Farmer Released by Benedict's Sight Alone

A certain Goth named Zalla was of the treacherous Arian sect.[69] In the time of their king Totila, he was inflamed with a passion of extreme cruelty against the religious of the Catholic Church to the point that any cleric or monk who came before him in no way escaped from his hands alive. One day, burning with greed for plunder, he afflicted a certain farmer with cruel torments, and he mutilated the man through various tortures. The farmer, overcome with pain, said that he had entrusted his belongings to Benedict, the servant of God, for he believed that this would snatch him from torture to life by interrupting the cruelty for a time. Then Zalla stopped afflicting the farmer with torments, but he tied his arms with strong leather straps and began to force him to walk in front of his horse so that he could show him who this Benedict was, who had received his things.

With his arms bound, the farmer led Zalla to the holy man's monastery and found him before the entrance of the monastery

---

69 The Arian heresy was started by an Egyptian priest named Arius. Arianism denied that Jesus is God. Specifically, Arius claimed that the second Person of the Trinity, the Son, is not God but is only *like* the Father. The First Ecumenical Council at Nicaea in AD 325 definitively denounced the heresy and affirmed that the Son is consubstantial with the Father. Nevertheless, Arianism was widespread in some parts of Europe at the time of St. Benedict.

sitting and reading. The farmer said to Zalla, who was following furiously behind him: "Look! There is the Abbot Benedict I told you about." With the insanity of a perverse mind and a fiery spirit, Zalla saw Benedict and thought he was going to act with the terror he was used to, so he began to cry out in a loud voice, saying: "Get up! Get up and give back the belongings of this farmer that you received." At his voice, the man of God immediately raised his eyes from reading and turned to look at him and the farmer, who was held bound. When he turned his eyes to the farmer's arms, in a wonderful way he began to untie the leather straps from his arms so quickly that they could not have been untied so fast by any man's haste.

When he saw the farmer, whom he had brought bound, begin so quickly to stand up unbound, Zalla fell to the ground, trembling at the force of such power and, bowing his neck of rigid cruelty[70] at Benedict's feet, begged for his prayers. The holy man did not rise from his reading but instructed that he be taken inside with the assembled brothers to receive a blessing. When he had been brought, Benedict admonished him that he ought to rest from the insanity of such cruelty. The man left subdued and never again presumed to ask anything from the farmer whom the man of God had unbound, not by touch but by a glance.

There is what I said, Peter, that those who serve Almighty God more intimately sometimes can even do wondrous deeds by power. For he restrained the ferocity of the terrible Goth while seated and untied the leather straps' knots, which bound the arms of an innocent man, with his eye. This event indicates by a clear miracle

---

70 By the phrase "bowing his neck of rigid cruelty," St. Gregory is referring to the constant Biblical refrain that we are a "stiff-necked people." Zalla had been stiff-necked by persevering in his cruelty, but the miraculous untying of the farmer's bonds softened his neck. Thus, the words of King Hezekiah to all Israel and Judah could have been spoken to Zalla: "Do not now be stiff-necked as your fathers were, but yield yourselves to the Lord, and come to his sanctuary, which he has sanctified for ever, and serve the Lord your God, that his fierce anger may turn away from you" (2 Chronicles 30:8).

that he received the power to do what he did. Now I will join to this story a miracle he was strong enough to obtain by praying.

CHAPTER 32

On the Raising of the Dead

On a certain day when the brothers had gone out to work the land, a farmer came to the monastery carrying the corpse of his dead son in his arms. Distressed and sobbing at the loss of his son, he asked for Abbot Benedict. When he was told that the abbot was working in the field, he immediately laid the body of his dead son before the monastery door and, distraught with sorrow, hastily ran to find the venerable abbot. At the same hour, the man of God was returning from working in the field with the brothers. As soon as the bereaved farmer caught sight of him, he began to cry out: "Return my son to me! Return my son to me!" But the man of God stopped at this cry, saying, "Have I ever taken your son?" The man answered him, "He is dead. Come! Revive him!" As soon as the servant of God heard this, he was deeply saddened, saying, "Depart, brothers. Depart. This work is not ours, but a work of the holy apostles. Why do you wish to impose burdens on us that we cannot carry?" But the farmer, driven by his excessive sorrow, persisted in his petition, swearing that he would not depart unless his son was raised. The servant of God asked him, saying, "Where is your son?" The farmer answered, "Look, his body is placed at the monastery door." When the man of God arrived there with the brothers, he kneeled down and lay upon the baby's little body.[71] Arising, he raised his palms to heaven, saying: "O Lord, look not

---

71 See 1 Kings 17:17–24.

upon my sins but the faith of this man who begs his son to be raised, and return the soul that you have taken to this little body." Scarcely had he completed the words of the prayer when the boy's whole little body trembled at the return of the soul, so that in the sight of all present, he was seen to be panting and breathing with miraculous quaking. Abbot Benedict held his hand and gave him living and unharmed to his father.

It seems, Peter, that he did not have this miracle in his power, but he begged prostrate such that he could work it.

PETER: It is obvious that what you say is entirely true because you prove it with the words you say. But I ask you to show me if all holy men can gain all the things that they desire to obtain?

CHAPTER 33

On His Sister Scholastica's Miracle

~~~~~~

GREGORY: Peter, whoever will be more sublime in this life than Paul, who begged the Lord three times about the thorn in his flesh and yet did not have the strength to obtain what he wished?[72] For this reason I must tell you that there was something venerable Abbot Benedict wanted but was not strong enough to accomplish. For his sister, Scholastica, who was dedicated to God Almighty from her youth, was accustomed to come and see him once a year. The man of God went down to her in a house that the monastery owned not far from the monastery gate. One time she came, as was her custom, and her brother came down with his venerable disciples. They spent the whole day praising God and in holy discussion. Then, with the dark of night pressing upon them, they ate dinner together.

When they had sat at the table and continued their holy conversation to a late hour, the holy woman, his sister, begged him, saying: "I ask you, do not depart from me tonight, so that we may speak until morning about the joys of heavenly life." He answered her, "What are you saying to me? I cannot remain outside

---

[72] See 2 Corinthians 12:7–10.

the monastery."[73] At that moment the sky was so clear that there were no clouds, but once the holy woman had heard her brother's refusal, she clasped her hands upon the table and bowed her head upon her hands to beg Almighty God. When she raised her head from the table, there erupted such great flashes of lighting and thunderclaps and a tremendous downpour of rain that neither venerable Benedict nor the brothers who were with him could set foot outside the door where they sat. Naturally, the holy woman had shed a flood of tears upon the table as she bowed her head on her hands, and through her tears she changed the clear skies to rain. That downpour followed so soon after her prayer and there was such an agreement of her prayer and the downpour that she raised her head from the table with the thunder. She raised her head and the rain fell at one and the same moment. Then, the man of God, seeing the enormous downpour and the earth-shaking thunder and seeing that he would not be able to return to the monastery, began to complain dejectedly, saying, "Almighty God spare you! What have you done, sister?" She answered him, "Look, I asked you, and you would not hear me. I asked my Lord, and he heard me. So now, go forth and return to your monastery if you can, and leave me." But he, who would not remain willingly, was not able to leave the house and remained in the place unwillingly. Thus it happened that they spent the whole night keeping vigil, and they satisfied themselves, while not yet in heaven themselves, with the holy conversation of the spiritual life.

From this event I say that he willed to do something but could not do it, because if we gaze upon the mind of the venerable man, we would not doubt that he willed for the same good weather he had in coming down to continue. But against what he willed, he found the miracle from the woman's heart in the power of God Almighty. And do not wonder that the woman, who had for so long desired

---

73 St. Benedict's conviction that he had to return to the monastery seems to come from *The Rule of St. Benedict* chapter 51.

to see her brother, was stronger than he at that time. For according to the saying of John, "God is love," and with good reason she was more powerful who loved more.[74]

PETER: I confess that what you say pleases me greatly.

---
74 See 1 John 4:8.

CHAPTER 34

On the Vision of His Sister's Soul and How It Departed from Her Body

~~~~~

GREGORY: The next day, the venerable woman returned to her monastery and the man of God to his monastery. Three days later, standing in his cell, he saw with his own eyes his sister's soul pass from her body, be raised into the sky, and enter into heaven's hidden places in the form of a dove. Rejoicing at her great glory, he gave thanks to Almighty God with hymns and praises, and he announced her departure to the brothers, whom he immediately sent out to bring her body to the monastery and bury it in a tomb he had prepared for her. Because of this, it happened that just as their minds were always one in God, so too their bodies are not separated by the tomb.[75]

---

75 Pope St. Gregory is referring to the fact that their bodies are buried together in the same tomb. Today, their bodies are still in the same tomb under the high altar of the church at Monte Cassino Abbey.

CHAPTER 35

On the World Gathered Before His Eyes and On the Soul of Germanus, Bishop of Capua

~~~

Another day, Servandus, deacon and abbot of the monastery that was constructed in Campania by the senator Liberius, visited him as he was accustomed. He often came to Benedict's monastery so that the man might teach him about heavenly grace and so that the sweet words of that life and the sweet food of the heavenly homeland might pass between them. For although they could not yet drink them with perfect joy, they at least tasted them by their desire. But when the hour of rest pressed on them, venerable Benedict went to his room at the top of the tower and Servandus the deacon went to his room at the bottom of the tower, from which there is a stairwell to ascend to the higher rooms. Before the tower there was a larger dwelling in which each disciple slept.

The man of God, Benedict, eager for vigils, arrived early for the time of night prayer while the brothers still rested, and he stood at the window, praying to God Almighty in the dark of midnight. Suddenly, he saw light spread out and brightening all the darkness of night. It shone forth with such splendid clarity that the light which radiated through the darkness would have conquered the daylight. But a miraculous thing followed this vision because, as he said later, the entire world was drawn to his eyes as if it were collected in a single ray. While he had his eyes transfixed by the splendor of the shining light, the venerable abbot saw the soul of Germanus, bishop of Capua, be carried from the fiery sphere into heaven by the angels. Then, wanting to invite a witness for so great a miracle, he called Servandus the deacon with great cries two or three times by name. Troubled at Benedict's unusual clamor, Servandus climbed up and gazed upon a part of the light he saw already passing away. The man of God told him the things that had happened in order, and Servandus marveled at so great a miracle. Benedict immediately ordered a religious man, Theopropus, in the town of Cassino to go that very night to the city of Capua to learn and report what had happened to the bishop Germanus. It happened that he who was sent found the most reverent bishop Germanus already deceased and, inquiring further, learned that he had passed at the very moment when the man of God saw his ascent.

PETER: What a miraculous and stupefying event! But what you say—that the whole world was drawn before his eyes as if under a single ray—since I have never experienced the like, I do not know how to guess how it could be that the world is seen by one man.

GREGORY: Hold firm to what I say, Peter. Every creature appears small to the soul seeing the Creator because although the soul will behold only a little of the Creator's light, everything that is created appears briefly to it. For by that light of intimate vision, the opening of the mind is relaxed and expanded in God so much that it exists beyond the world. The very soul of the one seeing also becomes greater than itself. When it is enraptured above itself in God's light, it is amplified interiorly, and when it looks below itself, it comprehends in an exalted way but briefly what it could not comprehend while it was brought low. Therefore, the man who intuited the fiery globe also saw the angels returning to heaven.[76] So, what is miraculous if he, who was raised in the light of his mind beyond the world, saw the world collected before him? But when it is said that the world was drawn together before his eyes, heaven and earth were not shrunk. The mind of the seer, who was raptured in God and could see all things that are under God, was expanded. Therefore, there was a light in the inner mind in that light that shines in the external eyes. That inner light showed the mind of the seer all lower things, although they were small, because he was caught up to higher things.

PETER: It seems to me useful that I did not understand what you said because your explanation has grown from my slowness. Since you have poured these ideas into my mind, I ask you to resume the order of your narration.

---

76 See Genesis 28:12 and John 1:51.

CHAPTER 36

On the Writing of the Rule for Monks

GREGORY: I would willingly tell you many more things about this venerable abbot, but I eagerly pass over some of them because I hasten to relate the actions of others.[77] I do not wish it to be hidden from you that the man of God, in the midst of so many miracles by which he illuminated the world, also shone excellently for his doctrine. For he wrote a Rule for Monks,[78] excellent in discretion and splendid in speech. If someone wanted to know in greater detail his customs and way of life, he could find all the acts of his teaching in the institution of that Rule because the holy man could in no way teach differently than he lived.

---

77 This line refers to the fact that this account of the life and miracles of St. Benedict is part of a larger dialogue, which discusses several other saints.
78 This is *The Rule of St. Benedict*, which played a key role in forming Western monasticism.

CHAPTER 37

On the Prophecy of His Death Foretold to the Brothers

In that same year he was to depart from this life, he foretold the day of his most holy death to some disciples he conversed with and to some further off, declaring to those present that they keep silent about what they heard and to those absent what would be a sign for them when his soul departed from his body. Six days before his death, he ordered his tomb to be opened. Immediately, he fell ill with a bitter fever. His feebleness increased day by day. On the sixth day, he made his disciples carry him into the oratory, and there he was fortified for his death by reception of the Body and Blood of the Lord. Then, supporting his weak arms in the arms of his disciples, he stood erect with his hands raised to heaven and, with words of prayer, breathed his last.[79]

On that day, two of his brothers, one remaining in his cell, the other a long way off, had a revelation of one and the same vision. They saw a way spread with cloaks and innumerable shining lamps stretching directly to the east from his cell into heaven. A man of venerable aspect, standing high above, asked them whose way it was that they saw. They confessed to him that they did not know. He said to them, "This is the way by which Benedict, the

---

[79] See 1 Timothy 2:8: "I desire then that in every place the men should pray, lifting holy hands without anger or quarreling." See also Exodus 17:11–13.

beloved of the Lord, ascended into heaven." Thus, those who were not present knew the holy man's death from the sign that he had foretold them just as his disciples present saw it. He was buried in the oratory of Blessed John the Baptist, which he had constructed from the destroyed altar of Apollo.[80]

---

80 This oratory was destroyed during World War II by American bombing on February 15, 1944. Although a bomb landed right next to the tomb of St. Benedict and St. Scholastica, the tomb was unscathed.

CHAPTER 38

Of the Insane Woman Healed Through His Cave

Even to this day, miracles shine forth in that cave where he dwelled in Subiaco, if the faith of those seeking the miracles calls them forth. Not long ago a miracle happened there that I will tell you about. A certain woman who was out of her mind and completely robbed of her sense wandered day and night through the mountains and valleys, the forests and the plains, resting only where exhaustion forced her to stop. On a certain day, as she wandered in her madness, she came upon the cave of the blessed man, Abbot Benedict. She stayed there, not knowing whose cave she had entered. And she left the cave after her stay so healed in her senses that it was as if she had never had any insanity, and she remained healed for her whole life.

PETER: Why is it that we experience that more often than not the relics of the saints show more miracles than the saints do through their bodies, even in the case of the martyrs? And they perform even greater miracles where they are not present!

GREGORY: Do not doubt, Peter, that the holy martyrs are strong enough to show many signs where their bodies lie, and they do perform innumerable miracles for those seeking with a pure mind. But because it can be doubted by those with weak minds whether the saints are present there to hear when they are not in their bodies, it is necessary for them to work greater miracles where the weak mind can doubt their presence. But a mind fixed on God has much more merit of faith such that it knows they are there, not in body but present to prayer. Consequently, so that he might expand faith in the disciples, Truth himself said, "If I do not depart, the Paraclete will not come to you."[81] For since it happens that the Paraclete Spirit always proceeds from the Father and the Son, why did the Son say he was going to depart so that he would come who never departs from the Son? But because the disciples, perceiving the Lord in the flesh, desired always to see him with their bodily eyes, he rightly said to them, "Unless I depart, the Paraclete will not come," as if it were said plainly, "If I do not take away the body, I do not show you the love of the Spirit. And unless you cease perceiving me bodily, you will not learn to love me spiritually."

PETER: What you say pleases me.

GREGORY: We should stop our conversation for a while, so that we may prepare to speak again of the miracles of other saints.

---

81 See John 16:7.